PRAISE

"What a joy to discover *Naked: the rhythm and groove of it. The depth and length to it.* It's always a unique pleasure to discover a new young writer taking on loving though difficult subjects. Nastashia Minto is finding new ground. We are all so fortunate to be a part of this discovery."

—Nikki Giovanni, author of *A Good Cry: What We Learn from Tears and Laughter*

"When a singular voice emerges, you can feel it in your whole body. Your bones ring like tuning forks, and your heart leaps a beat or two. That's the kind of voice rising from Nastashia Minto's book, *Naked*. This language is true to a body. Threading through sexuality, family, the crucible of religious upbringing, relationships, and a secular spirituality that will make you want to sing or bring you back to a table with other people, the poetry and storytelling ask you to open to the ways in which we are always shedding skins, always reinventing selves and songs. Carrying the rhythms and brutalities and beauty of the South, these lyric flashes will remind you how stories can loosen the knot of history so that a body may yet become. Language made naked so that we might yet see—and remember—all of our becomings."

—Lidia Yuknavitch, author of *The Book of Joan* and *The Misfit's Manifesto*

"Filled with candor and bravery, Nastashia Minto's *Naked* provides an intimate look into the genesis of a poet—from family triumphs to sexual trauma, from defeat to transcendence. Minto's nascent voice is filled with ardor for poetic form, both inherited and invented, and blends visceral narrative storytelling with a rhyme-master's heart. Whether the scene involves kitchen mornings with grandma, or a queer body staring down the barrel of a police gun, *Naked* reminds us of the word to redefine a life of action; "Don't be still—take / charge of your show."

—SHAYLA LAWSON, author of *I Think I'm Ready to See Frank Ocean.*

"Nastashia Minto's debut poetry is naked, erotic mysticism and deep Georgia clay and Northwest rainforest reality. Written in a voice that wasn't supposed to survive and is, every day, in varying kinds of harm's way, this collection is black and gay and dreamscape. It's nightmarescape and moon. Minto is everything."

—JENNY FORRESTER, author of *Narrow River, Wide Sky*

"Nastashia Minto has written a book at once a love letter and a riot song. Her poetry brims with wisdom centuries deep, at times sage and bold, at times sly and sexy, and at all times loving and illuminating. She will transform your molecular design. How lucky we the world are to bear witness to her power."

—REEMA ZAMAN, author of *I Am Yours*

"In Nastashia Minto's *Naked*, you will witness the transformation of a girl sitting 'quietly at the table eating [her] black-eye peas and cornbread with [her] grandma' to a woman who stands up to police brandishing guns at a black man to a woman in love with a woman's 'laugh which...sounds like small streams running beside [her] face.' And in her words, you will find your own naked truth."

—KATE GREY, author of *Carry the Sky*

"Minto seems to catwalk through this book bare and unashamed. The very foundation of acceptance of self, of others and being grateful for all is astonishingly sensed through each piece. Anyone going through a transition within their lives will find Minto's words supportive. I find the works within *Naked* to be heartbreaking, healing, and unabashedly honest. I look forward very much to rereading this and more by Nastashia Minto."

—REBECCA SMOLEN, author of *Womanhood & Other Scars*

NAKED

The rhythm and groove of it. The depth and length to it.

Paul,

Love & Light
thank you for being
who you are!

with Love

Nataska

NAKED

The rhythm and groove of it. The depth and length to it.

NASTASHIA MINTO

Eldredge Books
Portland, Oregon

Naked: The Rhythm and Groove of It. The Depth and Length to It.

Eldredge Books, Portland, OR 97240
© 2019 by Nastashia Minto

Editing and design by Indigo: Editing, Design, and More

Print ISBN: 978-0-9977491-2-0
eISBN: 978-0-9977491-3-7
LCCN: 2019931574

www.eldredgebooks.com

TABLE OF TRUTHS

CONSENT FORM

Before Everything

On these pages, I slowly strip myself of who I use to be, how I use to act, and the things I believed in for so long. I began to evolve. The process was and still is scary. Who is this person I am becoming? My mindset has changed. My perspective has changed. Physically I have changed.

If this would have been me writing this years ago, I wouldn't have been able to tell you what it meant to evolve. To grow as a being. What *ethereal* meant. What it meant to truly be a spiritual being enjoying these human interactions. Truly loving someone or something unconditionally. Taking the expectations off another and just let them be, you, us, me. What it meant to share space with someone without feeling like it had to be something more.

We are taught that jealousy is okay in a relationship—it's healthy. But is it really? Or are we placing our own insecurities and learnt behaviors on others? I couldn't explain the depth and connection to sex, having sex, exploring sexual preference, and understanding my own sexual needs. I was always taught not to do it. Or shown videos on sexually transmitted infections. Furthermore, there were no LGBTQ+ sex education classes happening around the Bible Belt where I used to live. So, like the rest of us, I had to learn from a few different ways.

1. Porn—we've all seen it or scrolled past it.
2. Trying different things until I was comfortable with myself and the other person.
3. Unwanted sex.

There are many, including myself, who have had one or a few unwanted sexual encounters that they either haven't spoken about or they blame themselves for and shame their bodies. I want to open up the conversation so that we can express and embrace our bodies, our emotional needs, our sexual preferences, our sexual needs and desires. Because honestly, how can we begin to understand ourselves if we don't know what we really want or we don't speak about it?

In each section of this book, I want to freely share in love, light, hurt, pain, connections, and intimacy in ways that are welcomed, explored, and unboxed. I've unclothed myself on these white pages hoping that through my transparency you will see me.

I give you permission to see me naked.

GENESIS:

I was originally birthed to be me, but society tried to create me into what they thought I should be.

Openness

I never wanted to be naked. I have always been so careful
about what is shown to people—what I allow in, what
I allow out. But now I see it is a time to reveal the truth
so that others may live. So that others may show their
nakedness, too, in the hope that we all may see each other
beneath the surface and live.

A Hero with Many Names

From conception, she was named a statistic. Her young mother, whose habit wouldn't let her kick it. An overdose would be the way for the both of them, but she was named Persistent, and determined to live. Five pounds thirteen ounces, she came into this world a beautiful baby girl with shakes from the crack withdrawals. Left in the incubator to face the world alone. Her young mother couldn't be with her, because the drugs were too strong. The nurse said, "What would you like to name her?"

The mother said, "I want her name to be something beautiful with light, so when they read her name, they can't tell if she is black or white."

The little girl made her way through the first two years of school when the teachers named her Bad and Rude. She held tight to those names as her bad behaviors were being displayed. The principal held his straight face; with the wooden paddle, she was put in her place. Gaining her stripes—I mean strikes—that provoked the anger inside. She was told if she were a good girl, she would be just fine. Until they named her BIG 9 and she held that name true. She didn't care about the behaviors—she just wanted to be seen. So she got into many fights with children and adults. She wanted to fuck up things. She didn't care who was on the path. It was all leading to destruction. She wasn't the one for kind words, because really, who loved them?

At the tender age of eleven, she grew as tall as a tree. She was five-five and all the boys were five-three. She was named Piggy because she was fat and ugly. The behaviors were worse because she felt that no one loved her. Suspended many times because Trouble was her name. Even sports couldn't save her—just left her with many pains.

She was told she needed Jesus. Then religion became her thing. She preached hellfire, and Jesus Freak became her name. That was her identity, until she met Snake Eyes Blue, and for two years she was named Confused. No way she could be gay and a Christian at the same time. She was named Hypocrite, whose fence swayed the line.

Even through the many nights of crying, she was named Bold, because she fought for a dream that only she could hold. Life had thickened her skin and calloused her heart. She was named Love, and compassion was sparked. They thought she would break, and her feelings were cold. But she began to feel in the depths of her soul.

They wanted her to quit—she couldn't be saved—but she graduated college with no help, and they named her Brave. She didn't feel any of those things; she just knew she needed to be alive. She was named Life because of her drive to survive. She desired to change the world but didn't know what to do. She was named Transparent, exposing her past to youth. She enjoyed the feelings of speaking and changing people's lives. She was named Sharp, and her pens were the knives. She wrote and she wrote without diluting the truth. She was named Gracious, leaving love when she walked through.

In the beginning, they were sure she would become imprisoned or detained. But *I am here! I am Nastashia*, and I am a hero of many names.

Ask Me...

Ask me of the mistakes I've made, and let me pull back the layers to my truth. Many false narratives, but I'm the original carbon proof.

DNA soaked in cocaine and booze—don't know how my genes survived, but ask me of the mistakes I've made. I still hold her truths, although she tell many lies.

I cry, we cry, she cried, but she said we were all a mistake. Maybe after one, but after three, take responsibility for their place, your place, our place in this world.

Forgiveness seems to fall off trees like leaves in the fall, but even in some regions the leaves will stay on the trees, so I guess forgiveness will never fall.

Ask me of the mistakes I've made. I'll be the first in line, raised hands to account for all the shit I've put you through. Ask me of the mistakes I've made. You preached forgiveness but forgot I came from you!

I Won't Complain

The sky is blue, and the sun shines bright out in these country woods. The smell of sweet potatoes, collard greens, fried chicken, and cornbread escapes every crack of the small shack we live in. Grandma would make us go outside to play or stay in our rooms while she cooked because she didn't want us to run in and out and let the flies in her "delfond" house.

On that particular day, I walked around the shack like I've always done because I loved being outside, but I had to be careful because of the snakes and poisonous lizards around the house. I walked by the kitchen window and saw my grandma's face. A face of burden, hurt, and pain as she stared out the window looking past me. I knew that she was in a transformative state because she was also singing, and there are only a few times Grandma would sing and we weren't in church. I moved closer to the window—but still watching for the snakes that crawled under the house—and listened to her sing.

The words of "I won't complain, even when I can, I won't. I've been lied on, but I won't complain." The words that stuck with me for the rest of my life because through every hardship and pain, my grandmother did not complain. I made my way around the house and went through the front door. The smell of fried chicken and collard greens lingered heavy in the tiny living room. I walked through the doorway to find Grandma still standing over the stove with her left hand on her hip, stirring the collards greens while still staring out the window.

"Grandma," I said, "you need some help?"

She looked at me and said, "Yes. Go'n head and get started on them dishes so we can eat."

Grandma's Hands

The same hands that worked in the cotton and pea fields.

The same hands that slaved over the stove canning food so we could have something to eat.

The same hands that stayed up late sewing skirts and dresses so we could have clothes to wear.

The same hands that sat us between her lap and washed and greased our hair.

The same hands that grab my face and told me to never give up.

The same hands that couldn't write and eyes that couldn't read but she never stopped trying.

The same hands that prayed for us every night.

The same hands that fought tooth and nail to live.

The same hands that didn't recognize my hands at the end stage.

The same hands that lay across her chest on the last days.

Those are the hands that are keeping me today.

Grandma's hands.

Hanging Ropes

Beginning

The hanging ropes that hang from the tree. A noose, I think that's what they called it. Grandma and Great-Grandma were never fond of us going to play out in the woods by ourselves because of the hanging ropes. Grandma and Grandpa both loved nature. Loved the outdoors, loved their garden, but they also loved their family and wanted to keep us safe. How can we raise our children, their children, in a place where the ropes hung from the trees, knowing its meant to symbolize the death of our bodies?

Middle

They hung Christ from a tree. The ropes that were supposedly tied around his wrists and ankles before he went to be slaughtered, murdered by the same people who praised him. Nailed him to a tree. I believe the hanging rope that Judas killed himself with was the real spotlight.

End

We are running—I don't know what I'm running from or to, but we are running. The terrain is desert like. There are various-size hills in the distance, but how, how will we get to the top of this hills? A rope falls from the sky. A hanging rope. Thick Kevlar, durable-type rope, not attached to anything. We climb the rope and make it to the top of the desert-like hills, mountains. A place where the shadows can be seen. We begin to run again, and a young short girl with glossy gray eyes stops.

She stops and turns toward the shadow. The shadows aren't frightening, but they can't come past the hanging rope. Then a black-and-white bird flies out of the belly of the girl into one of the shadows. It turns into a human and climbs the rope. Then a cluster of birds' flies from her belly into the shadows, and they all become humans and climb the hanging rope. We turn around and continue our run through this place. Looking for hanging ropes and shadows because we finally could see that they were humans all along; we just didn't realize it.

Tired

Tired is an undeniable feeling I feel often. So many deeper
levels to the all-encompassing feeling of worry, defeat, hurt,
and love. It feels like a river rushing through each boulder,
rock, and stone. Every ounce of water finds an escape route
through the cracks. I'm glad it's water! Water gives life and
the gift of life may help me not be so
tired.

Collard greens
Cornbread
Cream corn
Black-eyed peas
And fried chicken.
The smells that filled the cracks of the small shack.
Grandma, Grandma's hands. Sweat on her eyebrows. Thick,
broad woman with an attitude to go with. Love, Grandma's
love. The love and care she put into making food. Making
sure we ate something. Making sure we didn't have to rip
our hands out in the cotton fields.

Rice
BBQ ribs
Kool-Aid
Tablecloths,
Plastic plates because Grandma won't let us touch her fine
china, as she called it. All the kids ate outside, adults inside.

Family
Food
Joy
Happiness
Diabetes
High blood pressure
Cancer
Congestive heart failure
Gout
Depression

Bipolar

Schizophrenia

Food, the food is always good. But no one wants to talk about anything else.

Hushed

Trust Me with a Trial

Do you see me fit, that I won't complain, won't be drained, and seem as if I can't sustain?

Do you believe that I will carry this load, won't hang my head low, and my struggles won't show?

Do you think that I can bare it all, stand tall, and put on the best smile with hope?

You have confidence in me not to drag my feet nor sleep? Not to be in pity or defeat?

To God, that you believe in me, that I will continuously wear a smile, head up high, hands raised to the sky, joyful tears fill my eyes, praise that will never end, a deeper love that will begin, my best and closest friends, the blood of my ancestors carried within…

I thank you because with us, you went the extra mile. I know it's a privilege that you can trust me with a trial…

The heat creaks through the tiny shack, creating a feeling of being one step below the sun. The smell escapes every crack and crevice in the shack. The steam rose from every dish that lay on the round wooden table were Grandma sat peeling sweet potatoes.

"Grandma, you need help with anything?" I said.

She glanced up, looked over her wide-frame glasses with a smile, and said, "Come on over here, Stashia. Cut those greens, but let me show you first."

"Well don't you just cut them like this?" I said as I gathered two leaves off the stem and rolled them together and cut them about an inch or two apart.

She said, "Yes, but cut them smaller. I don't like my greens big like that, and plus we gotta put the hammocks in the pot."

"Yes, ma'am," I said.

"Grandma, what you gone do with that cake over there? It's falling apart," I said.

She just laughed and said, "Imma create a jelly cake."

"What's that?" I said.

She said, "Why you axin all those questions, gal? Go check those black-eye peas on the stove."

I slowly get up from the wooden chair, making my way to the stove through the creaky kitchen with floors that felt like they could fall through at any moment.

I hear the BBQ sauce sizzling over the ribs in the oven. The steam from the black-eye peas with okra chopped inside of it rose and crept through my nostrils. My mouth watered from the aroma that filled the room. I turned and looked at Grandma sitting at the table with that beautiful tablecloth, the cream corn, cornbread with extra butta on top, and fried chicken around her.

I said, "Grandma, can I get a bowl of these black-eye peas and a piece of cornbread?"

She said, "Gal, go'n ahead and get some. Bring me a bowl too. Don't let them other kids see you."

I sat quietly at the table eating my black-eye peas and cornbread with my grandma. This beautiful pecan-brown, five-six, stocky woman with a stern face and a huge heart. I am amazed by the sweat that covered her forehead from tirelessly making this meal and the heat that engulfed this tiny house. She still put so much love and dedication into making this Sunday meal for us while singing, "As long as I got King Jesus, I don't need nobody else."

Reality Check

All I ever wanted was to be understood—the rough-looking girl from the hood who was set aside to not have a place, but yet took place and became first place instead of being known as a mistake.

All I ever wanted was to be pretty enough, so that I wouldn't have to make up for all the things makeup couldn't do. No matter how many people I screwed, they will still never know that pretty just won't show.

All I ever wanted was to be cool enough. Cool enough to fit in, wear all the stylish clothes and fancy shoes so I could fit into something that wasn't me, but I couldn't see because I was blinded by society.

All I ever wanted was to be loved. Loved enough so I wouldn't have to go looking in all the wrong places, sleepless nights, and countless faces, facts and memories that doesn't erase, dates and times that can't be replaced with hopeless words and broke databases.

All that I was seeking was a false reality of the true me. Questioning myself, like: Who's me? Doubting the very reality that was placed inside—boxed up, my individuality and uniqueness had to hide. Covered my body with baggy clothes so that my femininity wouldn't show.

Nobody would know that I was hurting inside with nowhere to hide but behind myself. I was willing to lead myself to death and destruction because I repeatedly told myself that no one loved me, because I didn't love myself.

None of those things were the key. None of those things help me see. None of those things. I realized that *all* I ever wanted was to be me, and being me means to be free!! Reality check.

Deep Like Rivers

Every day for two years, I called my grandma on the phone asking her when she was going to come pick us up. Come get us from our auntie's house so we could live with her. My grandma would say, "Stashia, what's wrong now?" We were living in a three-bedroom trailer with my auntie and her three children. My brother, sister, and I would sleep on the floor because there weren't enough beds for us. I remember being seven, and surges of hurt, anger, and rage ran so deeply through every blood cell in my body. And when I attended school, I would rage and force myself to be seen like a singular blood cell flowing through each extremity at the capillary beds. I'm glad my grandmother saw me. Even past all the anger, hurt, and pain, she saw what I could be. Her love for us ran deep. Deeper than the third level of skin, muscle, and fat tissue; she was the accretor pili nerve that made the hair on my neck stand up as she would sit us between her lap and grease our hair and sing us old hymns. She was the anchor to the boat that always wanted to drift away. She was about five-foot-six, a stocky, strong, black woman with a Jheri curl. She couldn't read or write, but she could count her money. After many phone calls and suspensions from school, my grandparents would adopt us. Take us into their little two-bedroom house with the large front and back yards. Green-and-white shutters with fruit trees all around. They would take us in and show us what love was, what comfort was. They would show us what we could possess in this world. They would take us in the waters where love and peace ran deep.

Growing Pains

How could we be with someone who doesn't like growth or denies it? Gravity confines it, and they use that to fight it. Inspiration lights it, hope guides it, but they still feel broken. Not knowing that they're already chosen. They don't move with time, so in their reality it's frozen. How could we be with someone who doesn't like growth? We try to break the ice, try to be kind and nice, only to be the one getting stabbed with the knife. Because so badly we want them to see what we see, feel what we feel, heal how we heal. Not realizing that that all comes with growth.

"I tell you this," she said with one hand on her hip and the other swinging in the air. "If you tell me why your belief system is the truth, then I will follow you."

"I just believe. I can't explain," I said. "I just know that what I feel and believe is true."

She interrupted and said, "Because that's what has been taught to you. What do you think of yourself? Of your power? Of your intuition?"

"Intuition?" I said. "I don't believe in that. I believe there is one true God and only one."

"But why?" she said.

"Why? Stop questioning me what I believe and why I believe. *Stop* making me sin."

She said, "I tell you this to help you think. Think for yourself, be your own person."

"I am my own person," I mumbled. I left her house thinking of the deeply rooted religion I had practiced for so long. I believed wholeheartedly. I had preached on stage about. I had confessed many times of my sins over. I had many nights of crying from my perverted thoughts.

Why am I doing this to myself?

Why am I doing this to myself?

Why am I doing this to myself?

I sat in my small room with wood-panel walls with tears in my eyes, and I said, "God, I'll tell you this: I can't do this anymore. Free me, please."

Evolution to Peace

We don't talk about those things. Forget about those things. Neglect the effects they have on our brains. We are supposed to be strong, carry the loads on our backs. Our heads, our legs are weighted down by the chains that stereotype us into who we are not.

I've watched those so-called demons take my friend's life. She fought. You fought. We'll fight together. A stronger bond can withstand harsh weather.

I want to say it gets better, but your next question would be: When? When will it get better? The cognitive dissonance is enough to make me quit. I'm sick, sick of all the people that just say pray. I can't seem to fucking pray the gay away.

Don't sway. Regardless of my choice, I still lose. Because all I wanted to do was serve God and be true. Not possible. Not my place. Disowned by many, then seen as a disgrace.

I can't erase the time when I was nine and thought about the first woman. I can't erase when I was fifteen always crying, always mean. Tried. I tried to fight the world, fight the urges to stare at the girls. Tried. I tried really hard to pray the gay away.

Even fasted for three days and three nights to keep my mind right. I can't erase when I was nineteen and it seemed that she liked me. I couldn't fight the urges to be closer to her. But you see, she didn't have the same thoughts as me. So in shame, I hung my head and lost a friendship that couldn't be, because of me.

I couldn't hang around her—that would make me fall into temptation. Impatient, "I know I will be delivered from my perverted ways," I said.

But I can't erase when I was twenty and I saw her face. My heart raced, fast pace in a direction that I was sure was not good for me. "Please, devil, let me be free. Oh please, God, save me."

The constant battle within myself. How can I dare love anyone else? Treat anyone else with care? Trust anyone else when I couldn't trust myself?

It wasn't until I was twenty-three that the thought of not being alive outweighed the thoughts of life. This can't be right—I'm a Christian; I'm supposed to fight. I'm supposed to be strong.

Wrong! The fight was constant, but I survived. I survived to see twenty-five, when my eyes—my eyes were opened. I have spoken. God, I can't do this anymore. I can't believe that Jesus is true. And if this isn't truth, then God, I'm willing to die right now to be close to you. Because I can't do this anymore.

To fight within myself and not live true.

And God, give me freedom and peace, because I know there is something larger than me, but if I continue to live like this, I won't evolve to see.

To be, what I am created to be. And at the age of twenty-five, in that small room, my eyes filled with tears, heavy heart. Freedom and peace fell over me.

EVOLUTION:

Watch me evolve across these white pages
displaying a more complex being.

Seeking Truth

There was a time when I missed the old me, looking back, searching for all my insecurities, because they were the only thing that secured me. I was unsure of myself because all my life I was told how I should live and how I should carry myself, so I never formed my own identity. Even though I was "saved." I was still lost, trying to find the real me. It didn't happen until I started soul-searching and seeking a deeper spirituality. That opened my pineal gland and showed me the Truth (Maat). Seeking wisdom and knowledge, trying to reach a better understanding of self. I had to be stripped fully naked so I could embody my new identity. Whoever knew that being free means to be me? Now I can live in my freedom, walk in my freedom, talk in my freedom.

Only dreamers like to sleep!

Levels to This

What I see is the levels of hurt, pain, and misunderstanding
that surrounds me like a thick cloud of dust. I call upon the
ancestors to guide me on this journey, this journey to finding
myself.

So long we have lived in a society that programs and
dictates the way we should live, eat, breathe, and even be,
but I want to be me.

What I see is the truth that creates cracks in the chains that
have been formed around us—to suffocate us, to drown
us—but like the resilient people, we are "like dust, we still
rise."

We can't hide in the shadows anymore—open the hearts or
doors to new levels of you. Unfold the truth that will carry
the sail. Don't let the river run dry due to piled stones of lies
and untruths. Even if there is a little stream, let the truth
run through you!

Blackness

I hated my blackness and all the trouble it seemed to cause. Pause. I can't have work or wear this type of shirt because I'm black. I'm not wealthy enough to have my black South face, facing North.

Am I chasing after unrealistic dreams? It seems that everything comes in waves, in phases. I must time it out right or I'll miss my chance. This society is a dance, and fuck, I don't know how to dance. Pause.

I put on my pants that fit a certain way. I wear my shirt tucked in because I should appear a certain way. I speak and enunciate all my words so that they don't know I'm black. Pause.

It's a fact. We have a million things in our mind. Trying to navigate through space and time. We thought our ancestors fought, but we're fighting the same injustice. Just a different time.

Let's spare them, but no one ever spared the people of color. Outlining and tracing the silhouette of everything we created to remix it and say it's all yours.

I heard that's a common thing they do. Steal from other people and make it look like it's theirs. With false proofs.

Black.

It took me years to embrace my blackness, face my blackness, and really appreciate every curve and dimension. Did I mention the estate and the value my blackness holds in this place?

Surrounding by my ancestral plane, they bring me great truths and laid-out carbon proofs for me to navigate this system. I miss them. But I know that their spiritual beings bring wisdom and insight in a very prominent way.

So I will stay the course and continue to light my fire, lifting it higher to go back and rewire our people and their mental state.

Deleting the false narrative we've been given for so long. Pull yourself by your bootstraps, but damn, none of us have boots on. Sing a survival song as the day carries on. We are taking this back!!!

From the way we sing to how we do our hair, let's pass the torch and allow ourselves to catch on fire. Never detouring from the original proof as we embrace our blackness, our truth.

Blackness.

He Walks—I Stand

Five thirty comes before the alarm goes off. This is an everyday occurrence. Allowing me to write and read before the thoughts of the day are jaded by the thoughts of the world.

Flipping through the clothes on the floor to find the unworn shirts and pants to fit the day, excited about what's to come, will come, or has already came.

He walks; I stand.

Seven thirty meeting every day seems to be the norm. What is normal nowadays? Why are there norms? Because we have outdated the latest things they call to be true. If not me, then you!

Time seems to go by slowly when life continues to move fast. It passes in a blink of an eye. Don't miss it; don't cry. The words engraved on my heart: I not only have to be strong but also smart.

He walks; I stand.

I need to look nice for this night. A little unchaste is right. They write, we write, I speak but no one stands. Every person has a phone in their hands recording the injustice of this black man.

The bus rides past as my heart drops to my stomach. I can't stomach this. I need to get off. Let me off, let me see, let me be close to this man who looks like me.

He walks; I stand.

I walk through the crowd and see the fifteen police with their guns drawn on this five-eight light-brown man. With no guns in his hand or waist. My face is heated from the disgrace of our race because everyone has their phones in their hands.

I can't stand the sight of this. There is something not right about this. As I walk past the three white people recording, I stood only a few feet away from the black man to make my presence say, *I'm here too.*

He walks; I stand.

Out of the corner of my eye, I see this white guy making his way across the street, headphones in as if this is just another normal day. He walks through the crowd of cops, and they had to put the guns away.

Only for them to draw them again when he walked through. Dear white man with the headphones, I saw you!! I really saw you! Thank you!

He walks; I stand.
He walks; I stand.

The police say, "Go the other way and don't come towards us." The black man backed away. His way is towards me. I look at him and say, "I'm sorry, my brother, deeply." With a nod of his head, I understood that language.

And I can only think that if the white man wouldn't have walked and I wouldn't have stood then that man would have been just another black man shot down in Portland, Oregon's neighborhood.

He walks; I stand!

Afterwards I texted my sister and brother and waited anxiously for their replies. My sister sent back in all caps "OMG" with crying emoji eyes. "Are you ok? Please, please tell me you're safe."

My brother is an officer, so he is no stranger to that world. He said, "I'm glad you're ok, but it sounds as if those officers handled the situation the wrong way."

He walks; I stand.

I said, "I wanted to reach for my phone to video this and show you, but I was afraid they would shoot." And with sad emoji eyes he said, "Sis, you did the right thing because they would have definitely shot you."

This can't continue to go on. This type of injustice is so wrong. Why can't we bond together and be strong? For each other.

I finally ended with apologies to my sister and brother. Because I am willing to stand in the midst of fire and lose my life to stand with another.

He walks; I stand.
He walks; I stand.
He walks; I stand.
If you walk, I'll stand too.

GAY

I guess you can say I'm happy as fuck. Because Webster defines gay as being "keenly alive and exuberant: having or inducing high spirits," and my spirits are always high. No lie, even the very thought of a songbird singing brings sweet relief to me.

You see, they say I can't be gay and truly happy. That's not a thing. The therapist says let me get into your brain and figure out what this could be. 1940s frontal lobotomy. Let's change the brain and maybe that will change things, not realizing it changed my personality.

Let's just lock them away, they say. 1968, the date when homosexuality was classified as a mental disorder. No order, they can't agree, you see. 1987 they changed it to sexual orientation lacking evidence with no presentation.

1990 is when they wanted to celebrate me, we, or us. They give a big fuss about the pride moving inside and being free. Maybe it was the crack cocaine that messed up the hard wiring in my brain to cause me to think in such a strange way.

GAY

No way I'm gay. My mama is gay, and they say she is going to hell for her ways. That's why she is the way she is, because the devil stole her mind. No way I'm gay—the devil won't take mine.

1999, the first woman I saw with blue eyes and thought she was fine. I was only nine and knew what I liked but suppressed those feelings because they can't be right.

In 2000 Vermont stood the test, as they became the first state to legalize civil unions between same sex. I'm impressed by the risk that this state was willing to take. I wish it was the same for the other forty-nine states.

But wait, Massachusetts went and did more. They were the first with a legal marriage in 2004. What a surprise to the eyes of people of the state, now if the fire can catch to the other forty-eight.

Now it's a race or a debate, for what's to be alive, California has done it in 2005. Making waves, this new phase is about to turn heads.

Then 2006 came and the supreme court in Jersey said: Same-sex marriage with rights and benefits. But then California's Proposition 8 dropped so much hate.

2009 Obama is divine or shall I say sent by *Gawd* to do a thing. 2010 it rings. Proposition 8 is unconstitutional with no debates.

Now my story is about to unfold because I'm in college as this nineteen-year-old who only wants to be a Christian and serve God. That's so hard when the internal conflict strikes and all I want to do is live right.

What a fight when I see that thirty-seven-year-old blue-eyed woman. It hung so deep in me. I can't be. I can't be gay!

Let us pray it away, they say. Maybe a little oil and be baptized, all lies. I went under the water gay and come up with deeper ties to the feelings I had before.

2011, don't ask don't tell. Obama publicly supports LGBT marriages in 2012. Oh well, I should be free. I should be me. But how can a branch live if it's cut from the tree? Free me.

2012 I came out about who I dated. I waited, but she never did. She hid, because she had to hide the truth from her kid.

I guess I hid too, because although everyone else knew, I never told my grandma the truth. It's okay—she knows by now, the long and fearful truth. I guess I thought she wouldn't love me, but her continuous love gave me the proof.

2013 came as a surprise when the court struck down rulings and now all marriages are entitled to the federal prize. All eyes are starting to come into focus. 2014 many doors were open.

The court has spoken, again the ruling against the same-sex marriage banned. I stand, we stand, all in glee when the boy scout's presidents remove the national restriction on gay leaders and employees in 2015.

Pause, let's take a moment for PULSE nightclub in 2016.

GAY!

We come this far to still be terrorized, terrified by the danger that lay at hand. I stand, we stand, but they shoot. I move, we move, but they barricade us—we can't come through. I speak, you speak, but they won't hear our truths.

2017 gave us all the proof, harassing men and women over the bathroom they used. Criticized and demoralizing my brothers and sisters from living their truth. This can't be true; tell me it's a dream so I can wake up soon.

2018 I'm supposed to feel changed, not ashamed or embarrassed by my truth, but I would be lying if I said some days I'm not afraid to walk in my own shoes. It doesn't matter how smart I am or how strong I may appear. They judge my ways. So even with my hands up, they still shoot because I'm black and GAY!

Thoughts and Desires

Thoughts and desires, my goal is to aim higher. Prior to the things I've been or once was before. I'm not competing with anyone else but myself. To reach heights, fly flights, and dive deep into depths I've never seen before. They say fear is false evidence appearing real. While I'm speaking real affirmations, empowering faces to look and be in better places than they already are. I saw the scars. Afraid to let people in because they sometimes seem to make the scars deeper. They say she is shy and timid until you meet her; bold soul grows old with every year that passes by. No lie, this beauty radiates through her soul like a fire. Most seem intimidated, but she only dreams to inspire, and aspires to be better than she was before. Encouraging and motivating the people to have faith even through uncertain doors—to unlock screens, face challenging things, and become uncomfortable but grow. Renew minds. Forgiveness takes time. Don't be still—take charge of your show. Grow through phases. Burn and rip out pages, and create a list that you desire. You've come too far, too far that's why your thoughts and desires should push you to aim higher.

Mother May I

Mother, may I not carry your load because it's too heavy for me? You see, I've been trying to carry this load for as long as I can remember. Please give me permission to be free.

Mother, may I address the root causes of my fears and insecurities? The nights I wanted to be held but no one held me. The days I want to be wanted, but even you—you didn't want me.

Mother, may I lay down my burdens at your feet instead of you burdening me? Closed toes, socks too tight, cutting off my oxygen supply to my feet—I may die. Because I'm buried in your burdens so deep.

Mother, may I lay my head on your shoulders or across your knees as you rock me to sleep? Instead of lying in bed crying at night clutching the pillow so tight to console me.

Mother, may I tell you of all the nights I kind of wished you were dead? At least then I wouldn't have to worry myself to sleep. Wondering who was going to be the next person to call me to confirm you were dead.

Mother, may I share about how long I desired to be a child? Ran away from home to home just to find a place to call my own. Only to find I was still alone. Having to be the adult before I was even grown.

Mother, may I share with you a confession? When I was nineteen, I dated a thirty-seven-year-old woman who asked if I was experimenting to gain some lessons. Ouch! I guess she thought I was too young to love someone and needed someone else's approvals and blessings.

Mother, may I ask of the deep scars that engulf you? Defense is so thick, it's hard to love you. Lack of trust of yourself and others sometimes it's hard to hug you, without you crying.

Mother, may I say I saw so much of myself in you—that's why I was afraid! Afraid to be anything like you. I couldn't let it be true. I had to run from the DNA that created me because it was mostly you.

Mother, may I say that even in all of this, behind all your scars, in the weight of all your burdens, I still see your pure heart? Your desire to be more than what was offered to you, but not knowing how to reach it.

Mother, may I love on you in a way that is pure and true? So that when someone else tries to love you that way, you will be more open to receive it than to feel like you're being deceived by it because of your previous scars.

Mother, may I be honest to say I love you with a depth I've never felt before? Maybe because I feel like you're my child instead of the other way around. You have taught me things I wouldn't have learned anywhere else. And for that, I deeply love and cherish you.

Mother, may I be granted the permission to be free? Free of all the worry and anxiety. Free to have that childlike innocence and even laugh without feeling like I need to be more mature. Free from calls saying, "She has overdosed," only for me to say, "Are you sure?" Because, Mother, I deeply love and cherish you.

Mother, may I say that my heart would be completely broken if something were to happen to you? Because even in my burdened state, you still have so much to offer this place. And I desire to see your potential and greatness shine through because, Mother, I deeply love and cherish you.

But, Mother,
But, Mother,
may I be your child from here on out? Because now I'm tired.
Mother, may I,
please?

Daniel Drangonetti

I sat at the table with a few people I knew. Listened to all the people say beautiful things, read beautiful quotes, and sing beautiful songs. My legs shook because I wanted to speak. I wanted to say something. But I couldn't get up. I couldn't make myself get up. The conversation that ran through my head! I fucking hate drugs. Drugs tried to take me out this world before I even had a chance to introduce myself. Drugs took a few of my family members' minds, but they say we have a choice. Drugs!

Drugs got my ex locked up for fourteen years for illegally trafficking for a man she supposedly loved. Drugs!

Fuck drugs and all the shit it comes with. Antidepressant, I hear—when does this shit supposed to kick in? I feel worst or the same. Nothing has changed; two weeks later I am happy, singing songs. Three weeks later I think I can live now—I don't need these drugs! Kick them to the curb; don't look back as the sunny skies turn back to gray, or maybe that's just Portland, they say. Drugs!

Daniel, I remember the drugs, but I saw you the most. That smile you carried. The way you made people feel. The hard work and determination you gave. The encouragement you gave to other people.

Daniel, music lit up your soul like putting gasoline on an already-lit campfire.

And yet I'm sitting here, can't make my way up to say any of those words. I just want to bask in these lovely moments that others are sharing.

Daniel, you are everything, in everything, with everything, and I know that you would have loved to be here to read my book, but you're not. You get to inspire and watch me write it. I will forever remember and say your name. I love you, my gentle soul.

Daniel Drangonetti.

Depressive State

We've been taught about all fifty states, but no one ever wants to address this place. The one that borders many lines, loses track of time and sleep because of the darkness that encases its street. Streetlights, night lamps, and even soft ambiance won't help in this state. It sedates its residents with a heaviness that is evident in this case.

Give them vitamin D, or C, or something that will make them happy inside to enjoy the ride of this oh-so-isolated place. Or maybe antidepressants will make them cope with their stay. How long do you think it will take before they step off the ferry ride and ease into the groove of the chemicals? It could take days. What do we do, then, to help them enjoy their stay?

I hear the words of the men and women working next to me, and they say can a staff member also be a resident of this state?

We lie in the bed with the covers over our heads dreading the light that might peek through the drawn shades. We lie thinking about the nothingness that we feel for this day. We toss and we turn in our head without even moving. Nothing is improving.

"You shouldn't be in this state," they say. "You're strong, you've seen harder days, longer nights. The fight. You've fought, before you were even born. This state should be a piece of cake for you to chew and swallow."

That's shallow, to think that this state can be bypassed by any resident because of the experiences life has thrown their way. Is it a fair assessment to judge a resident by a house that is only supposed to protect the content that is inside?

Permission

His shadow lingered heavy on the gravel track we walked on late that night. He told me he was twenty-one and excited to be in the states. Excited to see what this new college adventure would be about. We walked through the soggy grass across the soccer field to my four-door green Honda. The darkness closed in around us. I didn't feel as safe as I had under the moonlight, with my seat belt on. He reached across and kissed my face with no permission. Why did you do that? I said. I thought that's what you wanted, he said. No, I said. Just because we're in the dark doesn't mean I'm supposed to reveal myself to you.

Darkness

Darkness—everything is dark. I hear the dogs barking, and I can't seem to outrun them. Two black Dobermans. Don't look back; just keep running. My legs—they have my legs. I feel the sharp canine teeth rip through my ankles; I can't move. They stop. There he stands, so close to me, I can feel my breath leave as his hands enclose around my neck. The sweat is salty. It burns my eyes. The hands, his hands, her hands, continue to shake my arms to wake me up from that dream. I scream, I'm dead—he's here; I can feel him. He is here. She climbs in the bed next to me and holds me tight, tears have no end, and sleep can't be found. She holds on to me for dear life as my body shakes in fear. She hums old songs to soothe me. She turns on all the lights to clear out the darkness.

Boxed

I think she thought that because we're girls, we knew how to do this thing. Maneuver through the game and teach each other plays. But there are so many ways for this game to be played.

I knew my box came with instructions and a label and so did hers. But that doesn't matter when you think you're in love and forget to handle the person according to the label on her box.

Oh, I knew how to love her, treat her, and please her, because I treated myself right. Right? Wrong! We heard that same old song being played on repeat, to repeat the defeat of the last breakup…

Boxed…

She said, "Just touch me and please me in this way. Caress my mind, body, and soul like this! And that will make me feel good." While she was forgetting to address the small details her label came with that said don't caress or press this way due to scars and deep triggers.

We figured we could press those buttons anyway. Why pay attention to the label when we couldn't even get in the box. Secure with locks from previous scars.

She said, "I'll treat you like the content inside of me, because that's what I know how to do. And the only way for me to feel is to provoke anger from you."

"Oh no," I said, "it's my turn to move in this game. That's not how I do things so you can't touch the content in my box. I'll shield, protect, and correct you before you get to scar my items."

Why fight her? I thought we were playing the same game. Boxed!

I've rocked that boat before. I was sure I was headed in the right direction towards the shore, but she made sure to remind me she knew how to play this game.

I refrain from the hurtful words and loud tone because her box had a big white strip of tape that read, *Fragile!* I didn't want to shatter or break the content inside because then it would shake me. Make me into something that wasn't even a part of my design.

Five years on and off taping and placing words on our boxes that would deeply ruin the items inside. We both tried to hide, with nowhere to hide but behind ourselves, which was leading us to destruction. Saying to each other, "You don't really love me," because we didn't love ourselves.

She said, "I can't do this anymore. I am ruining the shape of my box. I need to fix myself so I can be better for you." I was deceived by the wording "better for you," only to realize that none of it was true.

I guess the other girl's box could carry her truth. It wasn't even five months later and she said, "Yes, I do."

I couldn't believe it. This can't be true. I had hurt another woman I loved thinking I could unbox myself with you. What a fool. Even in this game, I got played.

I had to lay with the content inside, the worst emotional roller-coaster ride. Several parts of me died. Two years later and my eyes still did not cry, because I realized I tried to shape you into what I thought you should be. I poked holes in your box to make you more like me.

I couldn't really see—until I stepped away from the situation and saw the deep holes where cardboard pieces were supposed to be. The red tape for my box read, *Warning—Fragile*, in bold letters on the items inside, but I knew you couldn't see because even I didn't want to unbox the content inside of me.

Even I was hiding from me. I couldn't stand the fight of the cognitive dissonance I battled with every night. Wondering which part of me would win the battle this time. When your physical and spiritual doesn't match up with your mind, it causes immeasurable amounts of dissension.

It took years of repairing and replacing the content that lay dormant and fractured inside of my box. Replacing many labels and instructions for the next person, hoping they would take the time to read them all.

Until one day, the pen became the knife to the box. I wrote, on those brown walls, words that would leave me completely open. Took being shattered, completely broken, exposed to the world but surrounded by the universe to realize: I was never meant to be boxed!

Boxed!

Gaslighting

March had finally come around, and I was leaving the rainy gray skies, thirty-eight-degree weather in Oregon to head to seventy-five-degree warm weather in Georgia. I was excited about this trip. Not just because I was going to warmer weather but also because my brother's wife was having their baby. I knew how important this was for all of us, considering what had happened last year. I also was going back to see my ex, who I was dating again at the time. We decided we should get back together and try to make things work long distance. I get nervous about trips because I know anything that can happen, will happen. So, I braced myself for delays, bad weather, flight changes, or even the thought of the plane crashing. I'm being serious right now. I packed, repacked, and packed again because I needed to make sure I had everything I needed. I always carry several pairs of underwear because "you never know if something is going to happen" is what my grandma would say.

I couldn't sleep the night before—too excited about the adventure of the next day. One of my friends picked me up to take me to the airport. This beautiful Latina woman with her curves and sassy attitude stepped out of the car and said, "You know I love you if I'm picking you up at eight in the morning." I said I know. This girl does not usually get up until twelve. She loves me, and I love her. She has a kind, gentle spirit with depths that always go deeper. She desires to understand everyone in such a humanly manner. She wants to know the real, authentic person.

Our ride to the Portland airport consisted of crying and laughter because she was trying to figure out why I was still with my ex. Why was I holding on to someone I needed to let grow?

I said to my friend, "You know, she called me just before you picked me up. Not to say be safe, but questioning why I was coming because she didn't feel like it was for her."

"*Gaslighting*," my friend said with a sarcastic giggle.

"What does that word even mean?" I said.

"Gaslighting," she said it again and gave me her definition of it.

I had to google this word, because this wasn't the first time I had heard it. *Psychology Today* says, "Gaslighting is a form of persistent manipulation and brainwashing that causes the victim to doubt her or himself, and ultimately lose her or his own sense of perception, identity and self-worth." I allowed the words to seep into every drop of blood flowing through my veins. I had no words to offer after reading this, so I stared out the window at the beautiful lush green forest that lined the highway towards the airport.

She isn't gaslighting me, I said to myself. Why would she? My entire being was flooded with emotions and thoughts from 2014 when my ex and I had separated for the first time. I didn't know who I was or what I wanted to do or be at the time. I just wanted to be with her. Why wasn't she happy with me? I tried to do everything I could to keep us together, to make us work, but she wanted out. She said she needed to work on herself to be better for me. She'd said a whole lotta shit that wasn't true.

In the car, I could see my heart thudding through my jacket from beating so fast. I could hear my breathing becoming faster and shallow. My chest felt like someone was squeezing both lungs. My legs responded to the emotional overload and began to shake. I couldn't believe this feeling that was suffocating my entire being. Here it was four years later, I was sitting in this car flooded with thoughts and emotions. Didn't I learn the first time? Wasn't the hurt and heartache enough the first time? No, I guess it wasn't.

The car was quiet with a little background noise, and I managed to say through clenched teeth and eyes flooded with tears, "She is gaslighting me." My friend reached over and grabbed my hand, our way of saying *I'm here for you* without saying words.

We finally made it to the airport, and I received a text from my ex saying, "I'm sorry for how I acted this morning, be safe, cant wait to see you."

What the fuck? I thought. I texted back, "Thank you, I will be." I didn't know what else to say or do.

My friend parked the car and walked me to security at terminal C. I shared the text with her before we parted ways. She looked at me and said, "Nastashia, I'm here for you no matter what you choose, but you deserve to be happy."

I knew what she meant. I had heard those words so many times before from other people. But there is something difficult about letting go of someone you have loved with a depth as deep as the ocean. Someone who knew your past. Someone who shared in many traumas, someone who you allowed to see your scars, only for them to create more. Someone you let into the depths of your heart. You showed them the real you. You shared with them your fears, hopes, dreams, and desires.

You poured your life into them. Only for them to leave you empty. It's difficult leaving them, knowing they're the only person you want to fill you up.

I Hate How...

I hate how you make me feel. Or maybe the fact that looking into those beautiful eyes allows me to dive into layers of myself so deep.

You seep into the chains I have formed around myself to reveal truth. You gently approached my heart, understanding the scars and layers that laid awaiting to be touched by you. I hate how you knew that.

Drew back the shades, and the sun shined on dark places I've never seen. You smiled, my heart screamed because it made my body tingle inside. That laugh, that laugh which makes rivers sounds like small streams running beside my face.

You are ever moving and flowing to the groove. The beautiful symphony that is being played by the trees, leaves, and bees. You are amongst them—sing the beautiful melody.

You love the smell of me, covered in thick cocoa butter and men's cologne. I hate how we get along so well. Communication is an understatement. We truly allow each other to be.

In whatever state of being, we date the person that is most present at the time. We stop, fast-forward, and rewind time. We undress each lobe of the brain to find the time we first met. Maybe that's it. I could never hate you!

I just realize there will never be an *us*.

Scars

I look at all my scars, and they remind me of the places I've been, the faces I've seen, and the roads I've once traveled. Some of the scars bring back deep pains, while others are faint smiles. Then, there are some I just rub away from the person or thing they happened with. I can't change my past, but I can slightly dictate my future. I don't want to be guarded, but my entire being guards my heart with mighty force. I allow myself to feel deeply and love even deeper. Understanding the pains that may come with those two things. It takes a lot for me to cry, but when I do, it feels like waves of anger and hurt escaping my soul in a forceful way. These things I knew would come, because I decided to love you. I decided to be open and let you in. I decided to let you see my scars, only for you to create more.

Scars.

Triggers

You hurt me in a way that I would have never foreseen. Control, alt, delete scene from my brain. Pushing myself to sit through classes, knowing you sat directly two seats behind me. I wondered if you traced, retraced your thoughts to find me on the living room floor or bathroom.

My eyes strained through the work that should have been done in those last two weeks. But you spoke, and anger rushed through my core being.

I mean, don't you remember what you did?

Or were you just too drunk and stumbled on that fact that you took something I can't have back? I can't retract the memory of the pain and pressure I felt.

The pressure from the force. You forced my skin to stretch and tear in ways to accommodate your dick inside of me.

I don't think my body reacted how I expected, but you said, damn she is wet. Wet? I don't get it. My mind twirls in and out of darkness. Look at this, man, I hear. She is tight. As I lay on back, too intoxicated to move.

The room grooves and swirls with me. Please let me get up. I feel sick. Stop this. I move to the swirls of the room. I make it to the bathroom to release the content inside of me from both ends.

You win! I'll die like this. Misery. I can't even cry like this. Blacked out to wake up in my own shit.

How will I ever get over this? How will I ever face the day when my mind can't even comprehend what this means? I was too drunk. I made a choice. Is it my fault? This is my fault.

I walk through life with many others who have faced the same thing. Afraid to share, to speak, because it was me. I could have made better decisions, but that still didn't give you the upper hand to fucking decide for me.

I've lied, you see.

Just so people wouldn't know that it happened to me. So I don't have to explain, replay the memory in my brain. I mean, really, who would believe me anyways, compared to your statute?

You're married now.

You know what you did. And you never even apologized. Because the way you hurt me took six years to talk about. And for me to finally say it *wasn't* my fault!

Triggers.

Safe Space?

See, see, is this what it means when I'm told it would be a safe space? What the fuck is safe? For me? For black, brown peeps? See, see, if I was just in this place alone, I would be the token. Praised for my bravery to be. As if I'm not already brave in just being me. Waking up every day walking these streets. Surrounded by white walls, gray skies, and white people all the time. The only things that are black are my skin and socks. Meaning I would have to hang my head low to catch a glimpse of something that reminds me of my strength of me. Treading through the day with shoes on and not tearing a hole in these socks shows their strength. Maybe like my strength of treading through the day and dodging all the ignorant comments so I don't tear a hole in my heart, become cold in this heart from the passive aggressive people who look at me and say:

"Nastashia, everything isn't about the color of your skin."

Wake up!

The Escape Room

The words escaped her lips, and I don't think she meant them the way they came out.

We're sitting at a bar. She has already had a cider, and I'm just throwing back glasses of water. The food was okay for this praised place; we had to wait thirty-five minutes just to be seated. I searched the place several times to only find there was no one else that looked like me—there were no black or brown people in the entire room. This made my heart ache, but I knew that I also had to take into consideration the city and location we were in.

The words escaped her mouth, and I don't think she meant them the way they came out.

The question of "how are you doing" became shallow, and premeditated answers populated in the cache that threw my neurons for a loop. I'm so used to being connected, I lost the electrical signal through this conversation.

The words escaped her heart, and I don't think she meant them the way they came out.

Now my mind is in and out of the conversation. Staring aimlessly at the bartender and the half-washed glasses she served people. The words of "you need stability" and "stop running away from things" pierced the fibers deep within my heart strings, because here I am, finally realizing I'm not running away from something but running towards my dreams, but she can't see my heart.

The words escaped her, and they were released into the atmosphere. I don't think she meant them the way they came out.

I left with a heavy heart and dampened dreams. For three weeks nothing creative flowed from me. For three weeks I asked the universe to show me and guide me on the path I'm meant to follow. For three weeks I played and replayed the words that escaped her lips, and for three weeks my spirit was dampened.

The words escaped my lips: "I am on the right path," and I genuinely believed every word I said that was formulated in my heart and I released into the atmosphere.

I'm sitting at my writing group, and it's the end of the hour. One of my friends there says she have something for me.

The words of encouragement, inspiration, and empowerment formulated in her heart, released into the atmosphere, and escaped her lips, providing me with an abundance of sunshine to undamped my dreams. The conversation between three women, then two, strummed the fibers of my heartstring and sent electrical pulses through my entire being.

I clung tightly to those words.

The words escaped her lips, and I do believe she meant every word that she said genuinely and wholeheartedly.

She Said, and I Spoke

She said she hides her emotions because they run from ocean to ocean, even through all the fluidity she wouldn't want anyone to see, all the pain and scars because now the cuts are so deep. What used to be once a month has turned into every week. She said, Nastashia, can you help me? I want to be free. She said, can you imagine being a caged bird who has two broken wings? The only thing that makes me happy are the horses. I can't even fly to those things.

She said, you saved my life that night. You remember, Nastashia, in 2014 when I was ready to say, 'Fuck life?' I found a knife, and I was about to do it. But you said even through hardships, we can make it through it. She said, I never stop replaying those words hoping one day I would see, one day I would be unleashed into the world because every caged bird deserves to be free. Not me, not me. She said, I've been in this place since I was nine. I wish I was blind because then I wouldn't see the false reality of freedom they try to sell me. The attempts to bail, see, has only left me with scars.

That I wish I could go deeper, would go deeper—then I wouldn't have to be here. You know, Nastashia, when you told me you were gay, you gave me strength for another day. I knew you could have gotten fired and then you have would be gone. And the day you left was the day my hope and freedom went away. Your words made the days and months go by fast, and the light I could see, but now all I desire, Nastashia, is to be free.

And I Said

I love you more than a million words could explain, even in 2014 at the tender age of fifteen, I could feel your pain. Going from one home to another just to be caged again. Leaving you with questions of why don't you have any friends, why you can't hug and love people the way you desire. They said that type of gay love will send you to the hellfire, with no expiration date. I hate that I couldn't save all of you from that place. It's named a Christian ministry so no one would debate the strict rules. I wish I could have saved you from the damaging words that you heard. Instead of giving you wind to fly, they loaded you with rocks, broke your wings, leaving you continuously wanting to die. You want to cry, but can't cry because the well has run dry. Now all you feel is anger and hurt towards these people because for almost eleven years, your entire life has been a lie. From one abusive family to the other.

God, why? Why would you allow a child to suffer through that type of pain? First physical, then mental, now spiritually she has been strained. Or should I say, is chained by the oppressor's hands. As their words grip her by the neck with no desire to loosen the grip. She trips and stumbles because she needs air to breathe. Same cage, different age. Why can't I save her, please? From the people who don't see the cuts above her knees. This crazy thought in people's head that if we take their money and give them a bed, then everything should be fine. It doesn't matter if they're lying about the services they don't offer.

You are such a beautiful bird, I don't even know how they caught and kept you this long. From home to home with no place that feels like you belong.

She Said

Nastashia, I'm tired of holding on. I'm tired of being strong. It seems like forever is just way too long. I'll try, I promise I'll try to build my wings to fly because I want to taste of freedom like you.

And I Spoke

Sweet bird, I will always be here with you, because that's all my heart desire is for you—to taste freedom too.

Stiff

The pressure that surrounds my heart makes my body shake. Sweat escapes my armpits and hands. This feeling I've never had before—it makes me nervous, yet I'm continuously told that's how I make others feel. The fear of being loved, letting someone in, has stiffened me. Will this person or persons be careful with my heart like I am with theirs?

The Beauty of Being Alone

I thought I found myself, only to figure out I was still lost,
seeking and searching for something that didn't want to be
found. I wasn't looking for me or the thing I thought I could
be or would be, but what should I be? You know. Is it wrong
of me to set such high expectations? I'm tired of all these
low vibrations. No drug-use, mind so high mid-levitation.
Credential as healer, with no thesis or dissertation. Just
because I'm in tuned with the elements of higher vibrations.
Written in my conclusion to this time and this date, I state:
I aim so high, everything is at stake. Fail many times, but
what's success without mistakes? No fakes, big snakes
hissing around my throne. Transparent, solid, genuine
people—that's my community; that's my home. My dreams
are so big, they outlive the space in my dome. I don't have to
seek out others when I appreciate the beauty of being alone.

No, Not Me

I don't want to be another statistic at the age of fifteen, used up and abused, grew up in the projects because that's all I knew. I don't want to be another statistic strung out on drugs, broken hearts, no love, thick skin 'cause you know black women—that's always us. I don't want to have to feel like I can't create a space, have to change my face and fit into a place where I belong. A community or home, a safe space to cry on, cry in, and cry out to. The universe allowed them to pierce my soul, would make me bitter and cold when I turn old because I couldn't be what I desired to be. Old stories screaming pity, have mercy on me. I didn't want to be another statistic—that's why I set my bar high, failed many times before I learned to fly, and spread my wings on dreams and prayed that I succeed, exceeded the predecessor that came before me. I didn't want to be another statistic. So I will evolve in being me!

ETHEREAL:

I never truly understood the beauty of another being until I began to find and love myself.

Learning, Unlearning, and Relearning

I'm continuously learning, unlearning, relearning the paths and ways of this journey. When I feel that I have figured out something only to realize I'm still learning it. Churning it in the process of my brain. It's a funny and scary thing to know that something I've been taught all my life may not be true, may not be me. May not be you. When I come to this place of realizing the power I possess, the things I can create, the frames I can change. It changes me. I see. I see the things in such a beautiful way. Not a starry daze, or a confused haze, but the way the painter decided she wanted it to be. I've come to a place where I pay careful attention to all the things surrounding me, abound in me, top of my head, bottom of my feet, crowd and grounding me. The things that are surrounding me. The airy feel of the spirit world immersed in me. I see. I see. The beauty of the trees and leaves when I walk by the gray-blue of the sky still lights up my eyes, but I am able to learn, unlearn, and relearn how to love. How to let go. How to let go of something that is not beneficial for me. The process has never been a breeze—mind on loop, never at ease. I want to slow it down, slow me down so I can breathe. This is it. This is me. I am continuously learning, unlearning, relearning the paths and ways of this journey.

Spirit

You open doors that no one can open or close. You made ways that only some can foresee. You guide and lead in such a beautiful way. If we just listened to our spirit.

Yes, yes, we have to be connected first before we can even get to that spiritual level of understanding.

Spirit, allow your light to shine through so I can do my light work.

Continue to show me, guide me, lead me in the directions that I'm heading into.

I'm open, honest, and free to flow as freely as you feel, spirit.

I appreciate all of your guidance and help through this time.

I appreciate you never giving up on me. You never stop sending me signals or signs, no matter how much I stop paying attention, how little I show you in appreciation.

I love the connection we have.

I love the vibe I feel.

I love being able to sit outside and indulge in you.

I love you, spirit and ancestors. I love you, because you loved on me first.

Ethereal

You are like the pen to my paper, smoothly and intricately creating words to form emotions. Like oceans, you come in deep waves but pull back to give the heart time to breathe. You leave all creation fulfilled in ways that words don't have to say, but you emanate the presence that presents them with life.
You are life.
You hold a space and time that loops between fast-forward and rewind, but never confused mind because of the balance and harmony you seek.
You speak on all layers and levels of the cell, an anatomical being. You are keen, and sharp with many conduits to protect your being.
But you,
you chose to be the very thing that many of us are afraid to be.
You chose to be vulnerable and naked to reveal all things.
You are the highest spiritual being.
You are Ethereal.

Slow Reveal

I want my eyes to be as kind as my heart. My heart to be as sharp as my mind. My mind to be as tough as my muscles. My muscles to be a conduit like my veins. My veins to be as strong as my skin. My skin to feel as deeply and intensely as my heart does. My heart to be as beautiful as my smile. My smile to be as genuine as my words. My words to be as transparent as I am.

Mind Games

Mentally and physically, you can't reach me, so truthfully there is nothing you can teach me. Our minds should be so intertwined that we read on the same page. Thoughts on the same wave. Differ in age but yet the same age. Our eyes never disengage; our depth always goes deeper. I don't have to find her, but yet I seek her. Her love makes me stronger, never weaker. And in the midst of finding ourselves, we both found our keepers. And I'm not saying that we will be perfect, but to them that's what it would seem. Because they're chasing that false person of their dream. While we are living the reality of things.

Before I Met You

Universe, I loved this woman before I even knew her. Before I knew of her life story, before I knew of her drive and passion, before I knew of her pain, her praise, her smile, her happiness, her sadness, her way to cope and balance life.

Universe, I loved a woman who I had no idea if she would or could love a woman back, but the beauty of all of this is I loved me more than enough to be sure in her love. I loved me enough to not give up on her love for me, her desire and drive for me, her passion for the things I do.

Universe, I prayed that you would guide us together in oneness to create a very driven couple together. To create in this beautiful world to be everything that you have desire for us to be. Let us leave our carbon footprint on this earth. Let us be stars that shine all the way through and leave our stardust around. Let us be ordinary people who does extraordinary things. Let us use our talents and gifts to bring light to this dark world. Let us use ourselves to help other people. Let us not be afraid. Let us not be afraid. Let us not be afraid. You, me, us, them. Our dreams are bigger than just us. Let us not be afraid.

The Anatomy of You

There is really no reason to dissect, forget, or dismiss any part of you. Structurally, from the crown of your head to the soles of your feet, you walk deep in beauty and time. Unwind and dismantle the negativity that has been poured into you. That created holes, which caused the soul to be scarred from false proofs.

You allowed me to seep into your cracks that have been formed by the chain that bound you. You speak softly, gentle soul—love abounds in you. Mistaken, misshapen by the words of untruths. You accentuate every curve and move in your anatomy. It flatters me that you can be so bold but yet as delicate as the wings on a butterfly. You fly, I fly, we fly to higher heights and cast ourselves into deeper depths to find the anatomy of you.

I like beneath the surface of your soul—there is water where the seed can grow and the soil can be hydrated. Because we live in a world where the practice to watch something grow is outdated. We want everything right now but don't know how to make it last, but you hold both future and past. So, let me shine light on the brokenness of you, to reach depths that you didn't know laid true, waiting to be awakened or shaken by the light called truth.

First caress the features of your face and search every spot that you hold close. Speak to the insecurities and kill those ghosts—most parasites can't survive without a host.

There is no boasting, just toasting to the beautiful universe in every phase.

From those beautiful blue eyes, round face, and lips that speak life. That's right: you got the power; you hold the knife. To cut through untruths and let your story be told. Full house—don't fold. Be bold and gracefully reveal the whole you.

Not part truths, with fake mentions about your breast and what's between your legs. They're forgetting the mind, most times, and eyes that cry yourself to sleep at night.

Do you sleep at night? Still frightened by the things that have been left unsaid, still in your head, holding you captive from your own truths.

Allow your feet to walk trails, leave trails of traces of you. Generously giving copies of the original proof. Not asking for anything in return. But in return love, compassion, and empathy are graciously given to you. Every feature is accentuated by its own undertone. Even in weakness, strength is still shown. Not that you always must be strong, but to know that you are not alone. Your being has a place in the world. Offer space to boys and girls, women and men, to provide them with truth.

Like I said in the beginning, there is really no reason to dissect, forget, or dismiss any part of the anatomy of you.

B-flat

Our lips intertwine as my hands run across your face. I trace
the arches of your eyebrows. You smile. I see those eyes light
up like bright fluorescent lights. The sight of your happiness
brings waves of extreme joy and peace to my entire being.
Because to know a thing, and to watch a thing change into
what it is becoming, is what love feels like.

The small kisses become grander, my hand, your hands, your
face, my face, a place to hold our truths. Our shoes, being
removed and slowing making our way to the bed. One of the
places where this type of intimacy can be shared.

We lock legs as we stare into each other's eyes, moving your
hands on my hips, I unzip my pants. And you do the same.
Remove, refrain, from the items that may keep us constrained
from this symphony that is being made.

I stroke the keys of your breast; your chest rises and falls to the
beat. The small moans come in E minor played so beautiful.
My hands move down your pants, slowly transition to G—I
see, you like that chord to be strummed. My fingers deep inside
while I roll your clit with my thumb.

Sweet hums release from your lips, as I slide my tongue inside to
meet with the ocean. The motion, my hand from side to side, then
up and down. Your eyes wide as I strum your C chord so well. I
send shivers down your back as I sweetly whisper, "You like that."

You roll me over and begin to play my C chord—I like it strummed a certain way. First up and down, then side to side as you suck, you slide your fingers inside. My nails deep in your skin, I moan to release chimes in this beautiful creation.

Through intricate movement, we reverse time or sixty-nine to dive headfirst in the oceans so deep. You moan, I moan as we strum our famous D chords. The long strokes on our clits, we lick, both in harmony at the same time. You chimes, I chime. You move, I groove and the song is being created.

Waiting to be released into space and time, you chime E chord one more time, C chord—it's almost time. Our breathing is heavy, our legs shake, we strum the G chords faster. I feel our bodies quake. Our arms grip each other's thighs. You ride as I ride on the D chord so smooth. Our juices move, our bodies shake—we lay in this place to enjoy this melody we just made.

You move, I move, and now our keys and chords are facing the same way. Your lips, my lips, my hands, your hips, and you turn on your knees and arch your back and say, "Now can you play a B-flat like that?"

Stimulation

Stimulate my mind, caress every region. You never physically touch me, but yet you please me. Your words touch my inner soul and brightens my very being. Your vision enlightens my vision and gives me depth on what I'm perceiving. These feelings are not deceiving, because every nerve ending is receiving the information I am retrieving from your conversation! I'm so elated by the messages that are being coded into my DNA. That we can have a conversation and understand what each other is saying. It's like a beautiful melody that is playing. The words are so soft, they fall off your lip and reach my inner ear. Like a boat your words are there to guide everything that is formulating inside. My feelings don't have to hide, my excitement can show, my passion will rise, and it will seem like a transformation, all because your words are a stimulation!

You

You.

You take me deep. Not just emotionally, physically, spiritually, but all three.

You.

You open my eyes on all three plains. Leave me slain like or higher than the being I came in as.

You.

You know how to make it last as you open up my heart to uncover my past.

You.

You tear down walls, break through shells, and peel back the layer that is keeping me from seeing the reflection of you.

You.

You see the naked truth, straight through like nipples through a wet shirt.

Sometimes it hurts

Or maybe it's just uncomfortable, but

You gently caress

Each angle, untangle the webs that maybe forming around my truth.

You.

You know how to undress my mind and clothes all at the same time.

You stimulate every region. It's pleasing, you should *know*!

No really, you should know!

I grow,

I glow.

As your physical hand embrace my face to place the lips on
mine.
Your body reacts to space and time. Leave chills as you
caress the small of my spine.
You lock legs as our tongues intertwine.
You.
You move with the flow. The groove of your body with mine.
Lose track of time as
you place kisses on my neck then breast to make my nipples
alert. My hand slide up your skirt to feel that
You,
You are flowing like oceans deep. You look at me as my
other hand secure your back and my fingers gently slide
inside
You.
You like the ride or maybe this position. On top of each
other exposing the naked truth.
You
Bring your body closer, wanting me deeper inside. The
moans crescendo through the room.
You.
You remove my fingers and grind our clits together. It's like
warm south Georgia weather.
You.
You like the deep pressure and don't stop until we both wet
the sheets.
There is no sleep, only rest breaks and rounds to go.
You lay as your body relaxes from the sweet relief.
You.

You begin to run your hand from my chest to my thighs. My eyes and body react with sweet shivers from your touch.

You.

You love that so much as your lips and tongue dipped into my ocean so deep.

You whispered, she speaks to me, and slurp everything up and slid your tongue inside. I ride the wave freely.

As

You slide your fingers inside with your tongue flicking my clit. Oh, shit don't make me cum so fast.

I caress my breast, hold my breath to release this heavenly flow. I want more. Let us ring true.

Only to wake up and realize that actually

There is really no

You.

Soul Ties

All this time I've been searching and seeking for something I can't seem to find, rehearse, fast-forward, rewind.

What is it?

Where is it?

What have I begun? What have I done?

How do I break ties? Erase lies and create a healthy environment within myself? How do I continuously allow people to be, without hurting me?

Soul ties, no lies, it's deeper than most can explain, frontal cortex of the brain. Left hemisphere running off a right brain. Don't constrain, refrain from the things that draw you near. Vestibular, inner ear.

A balance

A boat

A steer.

Front not rear—be present, be here!

Feel, see, clear, spoken, and chosen, rewired, though, not broken.

You, my child, are the tie.

You know why.

Stop asking questions you know. Ask questions to make you grow.

Sweetly

I want to sweetly speak to your mind while my hands run down the small of your spine, leaving you open with space and time to open your legs and release the heavenly flow that escapes those pink ocean lips as I dip my tongue inside your openness.

Like the waves, you pull back. I draw you closer, pushing my tongue deeper. I hear the words leave your lips as I grab your hips and my fingers slide inside—enjoy the ride. While kissing your lips, remove my fingers then I slip these eight inches, so wet like a water slide. I grip your thighs and pull you closer, watching your eyes—this lovemaking brings you closure.

Your hand grips indicate you want me deeper—clit swollen, curled toes as I please you. Turn you over on your knees, arch that back, watch the spit run down your ass crack as you make that ass clap. Deep pleasure released through your moans—I could go on and on, from the way you taste, my hands on your waist, and the feelings you send through my spine. My brain on fast-forward and rewind. This is the best part as we release juices at the same time. As you ride I flirt with your nipples that stand alert. You squirt. It runs down my legs. The bed has now become our swimming pool.

rest break

get ready for round two

"You should come over for dinner" is the text I received. Although I was mentally drained from the chaos of the week, I sent a reply, "I would love to, but I need to go workout first and then I'll be over."

Working out has saved me a lot, along with writing and music. I've felt this type of tiredness many times before, questioning if any of this is worth it.

It is worth it, as my last client approach me and said, "Nastashia, you are amazing." I flashed a quick smile and said, You are too. My voice was weak—I speak, but it sounds as if I'm mumbling. It was hard to part my lips in that way, knowing how I felt inside.

I wanted to catch a ride with my roommate, but we've been so slammed at work that she had to stay extra late to catch up on notes and evaluations. She insisted that I leave some of my jars and Tupperware to make my bag lighter. I love when people think of me in the smallest ways. I went back and forth with her about it because I'm stubborn and I can do it, but eventually I said sure.

I started my one-n-half-mile trek home that I usually walk every morning with my twenty-five-pound heavy book bag containing multiple books, notebook, multiple forms of ID, a plethora of pens, and underwear because my grandma said you never leave the house without an extra pair of clean underwear. I could usually walk the mile in about twenty minutes, but this day it just seemed so hard. Maybe me being mentally fatigued was heavier than I thought. I found myself taking more breaks than I ever would have. This is unreal, I know I'm not that out of shape. I finally made it to my house.

Stopped by the peach tree outside to eat two peaches off the tree. They reminded me of Georgia. The peach groves that we would walk through as kids as you smell the sweetness in the air on hot summer days. The peach ice cream that tastes like it's straight from a peach tree and sugar cane.

I needed to pick up an extra pair of clothes and stuff for the gym and possibly to stay over at my friend's house. I begin to descend the stairs and felt the rumbling in my stomach. I ignored it. I will be fine. I packed a few extra clothes and buzzed the Uber guy making sure I had everything I needed.

I felt the pressure of my stomach now in my knees. Holy shit. Really. This is inconvenient, as I made my way to the restroom to allow my body to do its normal humanly functions. I get a text from the Uber guy: "I'm here." Why, God, why? I texted back, "Just a few." I really hope this guy doesn't leave me. I finished up, flushed the toilet, washed my hands, and made sure I looked somewhat decent. Grabbed my bag and headed out.

I'm about to get in the Uber, and my friend texted, "Hey, the food is here." I texted back, "Ok 10-15 minutes I'm sorry." She said, "no sorry."

The Uber driver is this six-two, very slender, redhead, young white male with glasses. He has books everywhere in the car. He said, "Do you like to read?"

I said, "Yes, I do. What about you?" As if I didn't already know the answer.

He said, "A lot, actually."

I said, "That's cool. Reading is good for us."

He said, "Yeah, you're right" as he talked about some type of comic book stuff that I just couldn't follow along with.

My gaze went out the window, which made me remember how tired I was. My eyes slowly blinked, initiating the process of falling asleep.

He said, "Is this the right turn?"

"Huh?" I said.

He said it again: "Is this the right turn?"

"Yes," I said. "Turn right here." I thought, he has the GPS and still can't follow directions. Gosh, we're so much alike. A smirk breaks my face.

I exited his car, and he said, "It was nice talking to you."

"Likewise," I said, slightly feeling bad that I drifted for most of the conversation.

I walked into my friend's house as she is super excited to see me, as I am her. I said, "Thank you for waiting for me to eat."

She slowly looked up and said, "Well, I did eat a little bit."

And I said, "Well, I definitely hope you did. I would have." As we both laughed. I said, "I talked to someone about putting together a collection of poetry."

She looks at me, as we both chowed down on some amazing vegan Asian food. Then she said nicely, "Have you considered all your options?"

I said, "Well, the publisher gave me a few options before they even mentioned their own company."

She began to walk towards her bookcase and pulled down thin books of poetry with beautiful covers on them. I turned my chair towards her and the books, but I felt a little disheartened. She said, "It's going to be hard, you know, but you can do it."

I slowly ate my food as I felt her eyes as they stared at me as she waited for a response.

"Talk to me," she said. Looking deep into my soul. Talk to me.

I managed to bring forth words without letting my emotions get the best of me. I said, "I had a long day and I wasn't expecting to come here and you tell me something is going to be hard. Everything in my life has been hard. Why am I even doing this?" My legs began to shake because I'm between angry and sad at the same time.

She walks over and grabs my face and said, "Nastashia, that's not what I meant."

I said, "I know, but I still wasn't expecting that."

I finished my food and made my way to her little tan sofa with floral patterns on it and picked up her guitar. I strummed a few chords for a while then laid my head on it as I strummed to feel the vibration. To hear the vibration of each chord.

Being in this position took me back to when I worked with a ten-year-old little boy who has cerebral palsy. He loved it when we played the guitar together. He would get all rowdy and excited to just strum one chord. That feeling flooded my body as I sat there with my eyes closed, head on the guitar, drifting away. Each chord made its own sound, its own melody, and it was so beautiful and peaceful to me.

I hadn't even noticed in that time my friend had made her way to me with a large pot full of hot water, and she said, "May I wash your feet?"

Although I don't follow any religion now, I remember Mary washed Jesus' feet with her hair. And I sat there speechless as my friend got on the floor with the large silver pot between her legs, her hair flowed over her shoulders, her eyes rich with care, love, and compassion. She smiled and said it again: "May I wash your feet?" I couldn't decline that offer—I knew this was a different form of love, gratitude, thankfulness, and being in awe. I was in awe. I was amazed by this woman. By her care, compassion, and understanding of where my heart was and what I needed at that moment.

I slowly took my socks off and said, "My feet may stink because these are my workout shoes." We both smiled, and she said, "I don't care."

I slowly immersed my left foot into this large tin pot, and a plethora of sensations rushed through the nerve endings, sending it to my brain to cause a motor reaction of wiggling my toes in the pot like a child. I wanted to cry as she applied deep pressure to my foot, but the tears did not want to escape my eyelids. I sat silently for a while because I was still amazed by this gesture. Then, I begin to play the guitar softly. First a G chord, D chord, E minor, and then a C minor chord in a slow strumming pattern. I had so many questions. So many *why*s, but it didn't feel necessary to ask or to know, but to just be in the present moment.

She said, "I know you can do whatever you put your mind to, Nastashia. I just want you to know that through this process, if you ever need anything, just let me know. I will be there no matter what it is."

I watch the words carefully form and fall off her lips as if I was catching water in a bucket. I knew that every word was carefully thought out. That she wasn't just filling air to remove the sting of the previous comments. I knew that her heart was genuinely invested in my well-being. I slightly titled my head to the right with a slow nod and said, "Okay."

I removed my left foot, and she wrapped it in a warm towel, and I slowly immersed my right foot into this lovely hot bath to flood it with heightened sensation and immerse it in the compassion that filled the entire space. I knew from that moment forward, the level of love, trust, and understanding would be a space we both forever held.

Anatomy

That song that I am breathing, you've already defined. Because you've intricately written every word on every line, which is released into space and traveling through time. You've opened up my mind and have begun to caress every region. Starting with the frontal lobes where there is logic and reasoning. Moving to the parietal lobes, which is helping you to understand what you're reading. Leads to the occipital lobes, which helps you translate what you're seeing, and the temporal lobes, which allows you to differentiate between sounds. You never have to make a noise, and I hear and feel when you're around. So, you've entered into my mind; now let's move to my spine, because now you know my thoughts; let's work on what keeps me aligned. Such a beautiful design.

How everything is kept in line by our spine, because of every nerve and muscle that it innervates. Our minds cannot conceive, because our eyes cannot perceive the perplexity of all of the things it generates. So that song that I'm breathing—you wouldn't be able to define, if you didn't have the muscles that are innervated by nerves in your spine. You wouldn't be able to caress every lobe and define every region, because the vagus nerve is what is keeping you breathing. So being aligned is very important for many reasons, but mainly, so you intricately write the song that I am breathing, every word on every line, so it can be released into space and travel through time, which can be understood by the complexities of my mind, and the structure of my spine...

Anatomy.

Soul Lovers

When I see you, I see me, pass the earth beyond the universe,
deep into the galaxies. So unique, very defined, like the
structure of my spine and the connections in my mind. The
feeling that I feel for you transcend through space and time.
You opened up, I pressed play and often rewind.
Not to stop time, but to embrace time, to remember and not
erase time. When I see you, I see me, beyond the stars in the
darkest hole in the largest galaxy. You are forming me, every
fiber and every being.
To be one with each other, to be one with myself, to love
me like I've loved no one else. That's how I will love you.
Like I love myself. Experience the world—you will never
be confined. Maybe redefined into the gold that you are
becoming, such a beautiful creative, innovative woman!
Your smile, your eyes, your mind, your heart are all a part
of the design. Don't stop what is being created, mind
transformed, reinstated. Vibrate so high, stay elated—that is
where we desire to be.
Because when I see you, I see me.

Moonlight

The cool breeze comes through the windows of the tent close to the small river we choose to reside by. The few trees would hide our silhouettes in, as the moonlight gazes upon our naked skin.

We lay on our sides tracing and retracing the beautiful outlines of the chocolate and vanilla creamy swirl. We begin with soft kisses, which elongates the sense of time. Opening up more space for our tongues to meet and greet, intertwine.

I suck on your bottom lip and hear the faint moans leave your body. Showing me you like that and welcome more. You reach up and grab my face to turn my head. Placing kisses on my neck as your tongue leads a trail to my earlobe.

My body reacts to your hands, your kisses, your smell. My body reacts to you. I kiss on your neck—I know it's your favorite spot—as your nails dig into my back.

I make my way down your chest and caress each breast equally with flicks and strokes of my tongue. I kiss all on your stomach to let you know how much I love it. You, all of you.

Your hands slid over yourself, as if you felt shame. I placed kisses on them and said your name. No shame ever. No shame! You slowly removed your hands, unsure of the sincerity in that statement, but you knew you were safe.

I place my arms around your thighs and pulled you closer. Making kisses down your stomach, on the inside of your thighs. Then I made my way to part your lips with the tip of my tongue. She sings in waves. I feel your body shakes.

Long strokes and strides, up, down, and deep inside. Before I pull back your hood and caress the sensational ball of light. I'll be gentle; I'll go lite. Applying a little pressure with my one hand above your bladder.

I take in the ball of light. A gentle sucking motion as I slowly slide two fingers inside. You begin to make your own motions, and I ride them out with you. I feel your hand push my face down into the light.

I take flight and suck a little harder, then I performed my ABCs, which surprisingly you liked. No, don't stop. Come back. Do that again. As I performed harder, deeper strokes with my tongue, I hear the air leave your lungs and your legs shake.

Your body releases my fingers and I bring them to my face, I taste, you taste and we both are pleased. You bring your face to encase my nipples between your teeth. I squeezed your arms and you make your way down my bare chest.

Tracing the outline of my tattoos with your fingertips. Slowly moving down this brown skin like you're modeling chocolate into a beautiful structure. I love it.

The gentle play, the kisses you make down my chest and my stomach. I feel my body reacting to every kiss you lay so sweetly on me. You kiss my inner thighs and my body shakes a little.

You bring your tongue into my galaxy, finding the milky ways, which make waves so sweet. My hand on your head as you please me. Slurping everything on this ride. Two fingers inside my galaxy, I released a low note minor E.

Please don't stop. But, I don't have to beg. Your head and tongue is playing its own song, and my chords are the ones being strummed. So passionate the way you watch and listen to my body groove and move to you.

You kept going—you weren't through until my body rose and fell to the strum of your beat. Your back, my feet meet, and I released moans. The moonlight greets and meets my orgasm like meteor shower through the earth atmosphere.

My body release the sweetness from the pleasure that I received. I pull you closer and I cave into the creases of your arms to lay way. You place kisses on my forehead as if to say, *That was amazing.*

I stare into your eyes and you smile. That small giggle that could move mountains escaped your lips. I kissed and watched as our bodies laid under the tent.

Releasing various colors of energy into each crevice of this slanted plane. We spent the next few minutes, laying, tracing the silhouettes of our naked bodies against the background of the bright-orange nylon canvas.

The soft whistle of the wind between the rocks by the river filled the air as we laid deep into the night. Long deep kisses from lips to lips, hands to hips.

My hands crept back down and felt those pink lips and sent chills down my spine like playing in Oregon's coast. I slowly made my way back down to your ocean floor.

As my hands embrace your breasts. I love this sight. Pink nipples so bright. Your being is illuminated by the reflective light. Such an unforgettable night as we enter again into each other's universe under the moonlight.

Naked

That small laugh that can move mountains and form rivers pulls back my hardcover shell and allows rivers to flow to you. I love to feel. I am so glad I can feel the depths and length of you. Stretching from east to west, I give my best efforts to ascend and descend your north and south pole.
Age has no limits, so really there is nothing as too old.
Unless we allow ourselves to put a bottle around the capacity and state that love should hold. I stand my place and walk this race, because we all know only those who endure will last.
I will take my time to smoothly caress the pain from your past as you do mine. To make sure we are not re-creating, or re-dating the scars that were left behind. But enjoying the beautiful symphony that is being created by time.
You allow me to see the naked truth and the naked you in both physical and mental state. I didn't break, but put kisses on each place that had been bruised, misused, and not understood. To take time to give you your body and power back, like real love should. Understanding that through gentle care and love, the process is what we make it.
Thank you, thank you,
For exposing your truths, because together we are
Naked.

ABOUT THE AUTHOR

Nastashia Minto is an African American woman who was born in South Georgia and raised there by her grandparents. She grew up in poverty and around drugs, alcohol, and family violence. Her life experiences led her to obtain an associate's degree in occupational therapy and a bachelor's degree in psychology. She has been writing since she was nine years old and has found that her writing offers her another way to help people. Currently residing in Portland, Oregon, she has been a featured reader at many popular local reading series, including Unchaste Readers, Grief Rites, and Incite. Her writing has been published in *SUSAN* and in the *Unchaste Anthology*, volume III. *Naked* is her first book.